STRONG WINGS, GENTLE WIND

By Raffoul Najem

With Asheley Clark

Contact Information:
Waller-Hill Publishing, LLC
P.O. Box 493
Tenille, GA 31089
www.wallerhill.com

10 9 8 7 6 5 4 3 2 1

Dedication

I dedicate this book to the two most precious gifts in my life, my beautiful granddaughters, Samira and Renee Wagner.

Acknowledgements

I thank my heavenly Father for revealing himself to me at an early age, and for honoring me with his faithfulness and presence throughout the years. I also thank him for giving me an amazing mother, Laure Najem, who instilled kindness and generosity into my spirit.

I thank my three children, Jennifer, Laura, and Joshua for their love and support during the writing of this book. I feel privileged to be their father, and I love them to life. Special thanks to my oldest daughter Jennifer for editing this book.

I want to extend thanks to my CCF family because their love of God continues to inspire me. They are an amazing congregation to pastor, and I am proud of the journey we have taken together.

I am grateful for the support of the two co-elders who serve with me at CCF Ministries. I thank Pastor Vi Whitcomb who has been a cherished friend and comrade throughout the last 35 years, and I thank Bishop David Karaya for his encouragement and stream of wisdom.

I thank my spiritual daughters Pastor Marlene Yeo for introducing me to Apostle Niegel Bigpond, Pastor Milagro Grullon for inciting me to write the book, and Donna Dougherty, my operation's manager, for her contribution and commitment to see the book to completion.

I thank my spiritual sons Lineu Zadereski for his creative ideas and remarkable design on the cover of the book, and Pastor Chad Waller and the team at Waller-Hill Publishing for consistent encouragement and support throughout the writing process.

Putting my life story into a book was a surreal and impassioned process. I extend special appreciation to Asheley Clark who wrote this book with me. She connected with my heart and infused life into mere words on paper. Thank you Asheley for walking with me on this journey.

Foreword

Some of the greatest of champions emerge out of life's difficulties and are molded through adversity and the crucibles of experience. This is the case of my brother and friend, Pastor Raffoul Najem. As I read through the pages of his book, "Strong Wings: Gentle Wind," a plethora of emotions captured my thoughts and heart. Although I've known Raffoul for many years, it was like I entered into a made for movie novel filled with much intrigue, suspense, suffering, pain, breakthroughs, and miracles. Yet, it's not some fictitious novel, but a real life story of one whose own real life experience is depicted with heartfelt and deep reflection.

Raffoul's story should provoke us all to a deeper life of faith beyond the superficial and complacent. We can become inoculated, even hardened of heart, and sit back on the beach of comfort and apathy while many are still shipwrecked in a sea of despair. I believe a driving force in his life is the constant sense of the needs of the multitudes still yet to find the salvation, healing, and freedom he himself found in Christ.

This book is filled with divine and providential moments, as well as miraculous Holy Spirit led intervention and breakthroughs. It gave me an insight into the window of Raffoul Najem's life and soul that also mirrors so many others who, through the crucibles of their own life experiences, have come to truly understand the abounding, great, and amazing grace of God…in ways many have yet to find.

Let this true life story of a true life champion minister to the depths of your heart and soul—provoking you to a deeper level of commitment in your life and calling and to a higher level of purpose and expectation in the Lord.

Doug Stringer
Founder
Somebody Cares America
Somebody Cares International
Houston, Texas

Endorsements

"I have known Pastor Raffoul Najem for over 15 years as a personal friend and as an Aglow advisor for the ministry in the state of Massachusetts. From the opening page, I was captivated reading Strong Wings: Gentle Wind, an inspiring story that vividly portrays the incredible journey of a man coming into his unique destiny in God. From war-torn Lebanon to spiritually challenging New England, the sovereign hand of God was actively preparing this man to be a bridge builder and Christ bearer between races, ethnic groups, and those from diverse economic backgrounds. This gripping story will draw you in from the start and cause you, by its end, to celebrate the faithfulness and goodness of God. Pastor Raffoul Najem is indeed one of those raised up for such a time as this. I highly endorse this book and can only hope for more!"

Sandra Wezowicz
Israel Education Director,
Aglow International
Watchman on the Wall Program Director

"I have known Pastor Raffoul Najem for over twenty years. I have watched him grow as a person and have seen his ministry multiply tremendously during this time. He walks in an apostolic anointing. His churches have had a significant impact in their region. They are multi-racial and multi-generational. To me, it is a true expression of what the church should look like. He is a man of passion for God and compassion for people. I am glad to call him my friend and I highly recommend his writings to you. You will be blessed!"

Pastor Mark Moder
Senior Pastor of Berean Fellowship Church,
Pittsburgh, PA

Relational Representative for Faith Christian Fellowship International, Tulsa, OK

"Eye opening and compelling, Strong Wings is the testimony of a young man whose trials and severe challenges in his beloved Lebanon were used by the Lord, who formed him into the man of God he is today. Strong Wings reveals the weaknesses and strengths we all have in growing in our faith and how they bring us to maturity in Christ. Full of insight, you will be captivated as you read this powerful story!"

Diane Moder
Islam Education Director, Aglow International

"Very few authors can capture the mystical hand of God and describe it with such colorful words. The rhythms of God's grace are seen in this unforgettable story, no doubt that where wickedness abounded amidst the winds of adversity, the wonders of God's amazing grace have abounded much more, to weave the strands of a glorious tapestry for God's glory. I applaud the masterful efforts of my precious friend and man of God, Sir Raffoul Najem and highly recommend this book. I thoroughly enjoyed this unique world-changing journey of a young man who was found by Christ and accepted the challenge to follow Jesus wherever He would lead. I believe God will use this sweet story to bless nations. May this true patriarch of the faith move in greater measure of God's goodness & grace to impact thousands upon thousands and bring a large harvest to the feet of a Jesus as he serves his generation in God's will.

Dr. Joaquin G. Molina
Senior Pastor, Spring of Life Fellowship, Miami, FL

A great story of FAITH against all odds that embodies the great TRUTH that with God, all things are possible."

Steven C. Panagiotakos,
former Massachusetts State Senator

"Very few people understand the Middle East, war trauma, and consequent life deprivation and dangers like Pastor Raffoul does. This is a great book that takes us on a journey back to his home country Lebanon in turmoil, to a new promised land America, then to challenges and triumphs of following God's path to building churches for all nations. Each chapter contains great stories and makes us reflect on God's miracles and grace. This is also a book for those of us who wish to pursue the Holy Spirit in our lives. We shall follow and be blessed by Pastor Raffoul's relentless joy and seeking His kingdom in his life. A very touching book to read."

Jonathan C Yeh, MD
Autumn Grace Medical Associates, Methuen, MA

"What amazes me is not the flying and soaring of big birds who cross the skies to the highest places. What amazes me is someone who has wings and chooses to walk into war-torn buildings, hide in the back of trucks, travel in fishing boats on stormy seas, jail himself in a church building torn into pieces, and with simplicity, overcomes all in a strange land far from home. My habib Raffoul had wings to fly, and yet walks humbly with God. Raffoul, you are an angel of God. You have walked so courageously. Now you can fly with your strong wings. I cried reading this bio as much as I was inspired. We have been friends for about 18 years, and his story is genuinely and absolutely true. Experience it! Be inspired!"

Josimar Salum, Writer

"What an inspiring God story from beginning to end. A must read for everyone who has a divine dream that burns in their heart. Raffoul, I love you and am honored to call you my friend."

Pastor Jonathan Del Turco
Senior Pastor of International Family Church,
North Reading, MA

"Being a close friend to Apostle Najem, I have no doubt that "Strong Wings" is a fitting name for this man of God. His life's journey from war torn Lebanon to the Northeast part of the United States has shown that the "word" given over his life was and is true even today. God saved him from war, personal threats, radical groups, and the disappointments often found in ministry life. This short book is hard to put down once you start reading it and is a must read for anyone who is facing challenging times in their personal journey and those whose faith needs strengthening. God has a way to bless and use you, even when that means starting from zero."

Rev. Dr. Cecilio Hernandez
Senior Pastor, Iglesia Cristiana Ebenezer Asambleas de
Dios, Lowell, MA

"It is a great honor for me to endorse Apostle Najem's new book. His life story and ministry has truly prepared him for apostolic leadership in the Church of the Lord Jesus Christ. His experiences and faithfulness have truly reflected his equipping ministry as a pastor/apostle, and his vision represents his love for the Kingdom and his understanding of the Church's mandate for these last great days. It was a real joy to read this biographical volume and know the full story of God's call on his life and to learn the fullness of his spiritual journey. I have known Pastor Najem for ten years and have recognized his value to the

Kingdom and family of God. His story and testimony is worth sharing and therefore, I heartily encourage both believer and unbeliever to read this book, for it is a powerful account of the grace, mercy and faithfulness of God during the most difficult of circumstances. Thank you Strong Wings for telling the narrative of your pilgrimage, for all who read it will be encouraged in their faith and better equipped for Kingdom encounters."

Dr. Ernest R. Henson
Professor

Apostle R. Najem is a Prophet of the Millennium hour. A man who has stood the test of time to be where he is and what he is. God raised him from a very humble background to preach the good news of the Kingdom of God to the dying world. He is a man to be an example, when Paul says in season and out of season. This book should be read by everyone. You need to understand that Jesus will never leave you nor forsake you. In Him, you are secure.

Archbishop Dr. Arthur Kitonga
Founder Father,
Redeemed Gospel Church Inc., Nairobi, Kenya

Table Of Contents

CHAPTER

1

THE JOURNEY BEGINS

Chapter 1: The Journey Begins

I washed their feet. Their tired, worn, and traveled feet, weathered like leather made soft from years of use. I could sense their initial trepidation and tension, but I would not be deterred. It was our gift. Our small and seemingly insignificant gesture of apology, but it was all we had. I knew that it wouldn't erase the years of hurt and pain or restore to them their land or tradition, but I hoped that God would use it as a miraculous spark that would eventually ignite a fire of reconciliation.

It all started with a dream. In February of 2006, a member of our church named Cindi Noon, a spunky woman with short, dark, wild hair and blue eyes met me in my office. "Pastor, I had a dream," she said. I was not surprised, as Cindi is a woman who spends hours a day in prayer and intercession and often hears from the Lord through dreams. "God told me that we need to apologize to the Native Americans. We need to stand in the gap and reconcile with the First Nation people." The immediate confirmation I felt in my spirit prompted my quick response: "Yes." At first, it felt like an impossible task, but the Kingdom of God is about connection. Just as eagles flock with eagles, our idea was shared from one leader to another, and we soon found ourselves connected with Native American leader Apostle Bigpond, the founder of Two Rivers Native American Training Center and pastor of Morning Star Church of All Nations. He was immediately intrigued by our idea and we started planning a Native American Reconciliation service, which would center on a public apology. Through another relationship, Pastor Marlene Yeo, director of Somebody Cares New England, we were connected with a man named Slyfox, a very important and well-known Native American tribal leader. He is a prominent leader of the Mashpee Wampanoag Tribe in Massachusetts and when we reached out to him to let him know of our plan, he initially shut us down. He responded, "That will never happen." His hurt and skepticism was evident. But after some thought, he graciously agreed to come and take part in our ceremony. We knew there would need to be a political element to our event, so we reached out to Senator Steven Panagiotakos. Senator Panagiotakos is a regular church attendee, and at this time, he was also the Chairman of the Ways and Means Committee in Massachusetts. He generously and miraculously provided us an official letter of apology signed by the Senate Majority Leader of the Massachusetts Legislature.

The day of the ceremony arrived, and the church was packed. I looked out over the beautiful sea of faces, some old, some new, some excited, some skeptical. There were members of the press, politicians, public officials, and familiar church members. It was standing room only. No one wanted to miss this historic event.

The ceremony was not long, as we wanted it to center completely around our apology. Senator Panagiotakos came to the microphone and publicly apologized to the Native American Nation on behalf of our state and presented Apostle Bigpond and Slyfox the official letter of apology. Slyfox could not hide the shock on his face as he reached out to receive the citation. He stood strong, proud, and resolved, tears shimmering in his knowing eyes, and he gave a speech of thanks, which spoke of years of hurt and resentment. "Thank you," he ended, "I have waited most of my adult life for this to happen." Next, Apostle Bigpond rose and took the microphone. He was like a tree, his feet deeply rooted in the ground and his arms outstretched like branches reaching to the autumn sky. Slowly and quietly, he started to chant, his voice rising above the crowd like an early

Chapter 1: The Journey Begins

bird piercing the dawn with a morning song.

One by one, his brothers and sisters rose and joined in his unifying chant, each one clothed in stunning traditional garments with colorful feathers and beads. Their heart song spiraled around the sanctuary and rose to heaven like sweet incense, and at that moment, a gentle spirit of forgiveness and grace fell from heaven. I closed my eyes, lifted my head, and smiled at heaven, grateful beyond words to be in this place at this historic moment. It was so unbelievable that I, a poor refugee from war-torn Lebanon, would have the opportunity to help facilitate this perfect moment of unity. I was so happy.

I felt Apostle Bigpond's strong hand on my shoulder, bringing me back to the moment, and I turned to meet his gaze. His laughing brown eyes were piercing. "Pastor Raffoul, I want to give you a new name. Your name will now be Strong Wings. No storms will overtake you." I took a quick breath. It was perfect. Apostle Bigpond lifted his lips in a half grin, a knowing smile that one might share in a secret between friends. But he couldn't have known the whole story and how perfect his new name for me really was. Only God and I knew the storms I had survived to get to this place, and only God knew the storms that I was yet to face in the years ahead. I shouldn't have been there. I shouldn't have been alive. But there I was, standing proudly next to one of our First Nation's greatest apostles, confident in my strong wings and in the Holy Spirit's ability to lift me above any storm ahead just as He had carried me through the many storms of my past.

My journey began 65 years ago in the city of Beirut, Lebanon. My father was a very strict man, and many were fearful of him. He had completed only four years of school, but his strong physical build and talent for working with his hands helped him find work as a marble, ceramic, and granite layer. He made a lot of money when he had work, but he was often broke because he habitually spent it all on what our neighborhood called "the good life." While he was generous and giving to others, he was also a proud man who loved to dress up in the best attire. My siblings and I were clothed in the same way, and even when we were short on money and could not afford to shop at the stores, my mother would pull out her noisy, ancient sewing machine and sew us beautiful clothing. Because of this, people always thought we were very wealthy even when we were completely out of money.

My mother and father are first cousins. In the Middle East, it was not uncommon for cousins to marry, similar to how it was in the days of the Bible. She was a very petite, sweet woman who respected and honored her husband. It was not easy for her to care for six children and keep her house in order, especially since my dad was not very helpful around the home. Whenever my father was unable to find work, my mother would stay up very late at night and work part time as a dressmaker, even after working all day cooking, cleaning, and caring for us children. My father did not treat my mother very well, and as I got older, I began to recognize certain personality traits in myself that were formed from observing the drama in our household. Because of the close relationship I have with my mother, I grew to dislike my father as I watched the way he behaved. I passionately resolved to be different from him, and as a result, I started to believe things about myself that were unhealthy. My father was a harsh man, so I determined to be kind. Unfortunately, I was out of balance. I allowed those closest to me to emotionally abuse and take advantage of me, and unfortunately, it wasn't until I was in my fifties when I finally saw and repented of my error. Thankfully, my mother was a constant, loving role model in my life. She is one of the wisest women I have ever met, and even though she never had the opportunity to go to school, she has memorized many wise, ancient Arabic parables, riddles, and poems. Over the years, I have come to love my mother's ways and have embraced many aspects of her life's philosophy. Her gentleness and meekness are admirable and while growing up, I saw that even in her suffering, she was patient and never complained. Instead, she smiled through her hard work and did all she could to ensure that we lacked nothing.

My parents, my grandmother, my five siblings, and I lived together in a two-bedroom apartment in a very nice building. Space was limited, but we found ways to live peacefully. Although I grew up in a traditional Christian, Greek Orthodox home, I did not know much about the Gospel. I was not really looking for God. I had no idea that I needed him at all. Nonetheless, His grace found me through a man named Dr. Elias Malki. He was a Lebanese native who immigrated to the United States after discovering Christ as his personal savior. While in the U.S., Dr. Malki enrolled in Bible school and after graduating, he felt compelled by the Holy Spirit to return to Lebanon to work as a missionary with the Foursquare Church, serving his own people. I am eternally grateful that he made that decision. For three years, when I was between the ages of fourteen and seventeen, Dr. Malki continually reached out to me with the gospel of Christ. His message was completely different from anything I ever heard growing up, both within my own traditional Christian background and among the many other religions represented in Lebanon at that time. Even so, I chose to make fun of Dr.

Malki, and my friends and I resolved not to accept Dr. Malki's message. In fact, we spent a year attending the church just for some entertainment. We pretended to participate, but we secretly mocked Dr. Malki. I even faked the born again experience by pretending to speak in tongues and making up spiritual testimonies, which I shared with great emotion in the church to impress my friends.

One day, my good friend Raymond showed up at my door with some surprising news. He told me that he had a true conversion at Dr. Malki's church and he shared his experience with me. I was stunned as Raymond was with us while we had been "playing church" all year. I was close to Raymond, so the news of his conversion made a great impact on me. It softened something inside of me, which opened my eyes to the message of Dr. Malki. One Sunday night in August of 1970, a few days after Raymond's conversion, I made the decision to accept Christ and become a born again Christian. After Dr. Malki finished preaching, he invited anyone who wanted to receive Jesus as his savior to come forward. He did this regularly, but this time, I rushed to the front with a flood of tears running down my face. My friends thought I was just putting on another show, but that night, something amazing happened to me. I knew with my entire being that I was becoming a new man; it was a tremendous life altering experience. I don't recall how long I stayed praying, but when I left the church, my friends were waiting for me outside. They expected that we would have our usual laugh about what went on that night, but I wanted to tell them about my wonderful conversion experience. I emphasized over and over that everything we had been mocking was actually real. It was real! They didn't believe me, and after that night, only Raymond and I continued to attend the church.

Chapter 1: The Journey Begins

The majority of the population of my neighborhood consisted of Greek Orthodox and Sunni Muslims, but all of us shared a very worldly, secular lifestyle. The evangelical message of the full gospel was not accepted at all. To some, it represented a western view influenced by Zionists who wanted to brainwash the minds of the Arab youth. To others, it represented a threat against the traditional values of the oriental form of orthodoxy. I knew that choosing Christ and accepting the message that Dr. Malki was teaching me would have significant implications on my life and even on the life of my family. It was truly a very decisive time of questioning my upbringing and holding it up against the value of Christ's message.

I had learned much from Dr. Malki and he had become more than my pastor. He was now my mentor, my father, my spiritual leader, and friend. Much, if not all, of my personal formation and spiritual maturity has come from the investment made in my life by this great man of God. I was 17 years old when I accepted Christ, and it triggered a change in me. Everything became new, and I fell in love with God, His word, and His principles. His joy filled my heart like nothing else did before, and I knew from the day I was converted that I wanted to become a preacher of the Gospel of Jesus Christ just like Dr. Malki.

Right away, I started witnessing on the streets even though the Islamic presence around me made it dangerous to do so, and I was often mocked by the fanatic religious Orthodox Christians. I was the first of my Greek Orthodox family to accept Jesus Christ as my personal savior, and my newfound faith was not received with open arms by my family or by my friends. At first, my mother was happy I was attending church. She observed the way the men in our neighborhood loved to gamble, drink, and womanize, and she considered my newfound passion for Christ a safe haven from these sinful lures. However, she slowly became furious with me once she realized the reality and strength of my devotion to Christ, and she began listening to the gossip about me that was spreading around our neighborhood. I lived through two very painful years of persecution during which my friends deserted me and called me all kinds of hurtful names. My family forced me to stay away from my new church claiming that I was bewitched by Dr. Malki, and mothers forbade their sons to talk to me. One night, as I was returning from an evening service, a few of my friends waited for me behind some concrete walls and they jumped out at me when I approached the dark alley. They slapped me and ridiculed me by laughing out loud, clapping their hands, and shouting, "Here comes the Hallelujah guy!" It was a very lonely time. I stayed many days and weeks alone in my room reading, praying, and preaching.

My mother feared for my sanity because many told her that her son was going crazy. Her initial support for my church-going routine had waned and in a twisted attempt to protect me, my family decided to physically invade my church to destroy it. A large crowd came to participate in the attack on Dr. Malki's church. I will never forget that night. Although I was afraid because I knew my family was angry, I was still determined to see them all saved. It turned out to be the most exciting night the church had ever seen. Because everyone had heard about the big confrontation that was about to take place, there had never been so many people in attendance at one time at our church. It was so full that people were overflowing out into the street. Dr. Malki preached a fiery message and the power of God fell on our little church building. We literally shook under the tangible presence of the Holy Spirit. Many people gave their hearts to the Lord that night. Unfortunately, this did not stop our attackers, and threats were made to bomb our building. This succeeded in putting fear in my heart, so I made the decision to stop attending church. Dr. Malki continued to mentor me secretly, and he waited for me every morning in his car at a street corner that was on my way to school. We would spend twenty minutes reading, praying, and studying the Bible together. This lasted for a year until I turned eighteen and graduated from high school. I secured a good job at the post office, and as the oldest son, I became responsible for providing for my entire family, as my father had become very sick. Eventually, I started working three jobs in order to pay the bills and care for my family. This was a heavy responsibility for me to carry at such a young age, but my new position in the family also gave me the courage I needed to revolt against my parent's wishes and the threats of the community, and return to the church. I also began attending Bible School at night. Even though I was dealing with a lot of responsibility, life was good, and I experienced great joy from loving God, His people, and witnessing all over Lebanon.

Dr. Malki had gained American citizenship years ago when he married an American woman, and due to the civil war, which started in 1973, and the dangerous political climate, he and his family were evacuated to the United States. I stayed faithfully ministering at his church and became the acting pastor. Over time, our congregation dwindled, and I remember one Christmas Eve when I was the only one at the church. A threat from radical Muslims had been issued that any church that chose to open that day would be bombed. My mother pleaded with me to stay home, but I was determined to celebrate Jesus on His birthday. I opened the church and even though the threat succeeded in keeping everyone away, I led worship, preached a sermon, collected the offering, and gave an altar call anyway. I felt led by God to continue the service as if it had full attendance, and I was surprised at how happy and fulfilled it made me even though I was alone. I didn't know it at that time, but God was using these moments to prepare me for His plans for my future.

The Massachusetts State Senate

Resolutions

MEMORIALIZING THE CONGRESS OF THE UNITED STATES TO PASS SENATE JOINT
RESOLUTION 15 APOLOGIZING TO ALL NATIVE AMERICAN PEOPLES
ON BEHALF OF THE UNITED STATES.

WHEREAS, THROUGHOUT HISTORY, THE COMMONWEALTH OF MASSACHUSETTS HAS BEEN INSTRUMENTAL IN THE STRUGGLE TO ESTABLISH DEMOCRACY AND SECURE THE RIGHTS AND LIBERTIES OF AMERICANS; AND

WHEREAS, THE DECLARATION OF RIGHTS OF THE COMMONWEALTH OF MASSACHUSETTS WAS THE FIRST ENUMERATION OF CIVIL RIGHTS AND LIBERTIES BY AMERICANS, WHICH SERVED AS A MODEL FOR THE UNITED STATES CONSTITUTION AND BILL OF RIGHTS; AND

WHEREAS, THE COMMONWEALTH OF MASSACHUSETTS HAS A RICH NATIVE AMERICAN HISTORY WITH INDIGENOUS TRIBES SUCH AS MASSACHUSET FROM SUFFOLK COUNTY, THE NIPMUC FROM CENTRAL MASSACHUSETTS, THE STOCKBRIDGE FROM BERKSHIRE COUNTY AND THE WAMPANOAG FROM CAPE COD AND THE ISLANDS; AND

WHEREAS, THE COMMONWEALTH OF MASSACHUSETTS ACKNOWLEDGES THE LONG HISTORY OF OFFICIAL DEPREDATIONS AND ILL-CONCEIVED POLICIES BY THE UNITED STATES GOVERNMENT REGARDING NATIVE AMERICAN TRIBES AND BELIEVES THAT THE CONGRESS OF THE UNITED STATES SHOULD OFFER AN APOLOGY TO ALL NATIVE PEOPLES ON BEHALF OF THE UNITED STATES; AND

WHEREAS, THE ANCESTORS OF TODAY'S NATIVE PEOPLES HAVE INHABITED THE LAND OF THE PRESENT-DAY UNITED STATES SINCE TIME IMMEMORIAL AND FOR THOUSANDS OF YEARS BEFORE THE ARRIVAL OF PEOPLES OF EUROPEAN ORIGIN; AND

WHEREAS, THE NATIVE PEOPLES HAVE FOR MILLENNIA HONORED, PROTECTED AND STEWARDED THIS LAND THAT WE CHERISH; AND

WHEREAS, THE UNITED STATES GOVERNMENT HAS VIOLATED MANY OF THE TREATIES RATIFIED BY CONGRESS AND OTHER DIPLOMATIC AGREEMENTS WITH NATIVE AMERICAN TRIBES; AND

WHEREAS, DESPITE CONTINUING MALTREATMENT OF NATIVE PEOPLES BY THE UNITED STATES, THE NATIVE PEOPLES HAVE REMAINED COMMITTED TO THE PROTECTION OF THIS GREAT LAND, AS EVIDENCED BY THE FACT THAT, ON A PER CAPITA BASIS, MORE NATIVE PEOPLE HAVE SERVED IN THE UNITED STATES ARMED FORCES AND PLACED THEMSELVES IN HARM'S WAY IN DEFENSE OF THE UNITED STATES IN EVERY MAJOR MILITARY CONFLICT THAN ANY OTHER ETHNIC GROUP; AND

WHEREAS, NATIVE PEOPLES ARE ENDOWED BY THEIR CREATOR WITH CERTAIN UNALIENABLE RIGHTS, AND THAT AMONG THOSE ARE LIFE, LIBERTY, AND THE PURSUIT OF HAPPINESS; NOW THEREFORE BE IT

RESOLVED, THAT THE MASSACHUSETTS SENATE HEREBY URGES THE SENATE AND HOUSE OF REPRESENTATIVES OF THE UNITED STATES TO PASS, PENDING SENATE JOINT RESOLUTION 15, APOLOGIZING TO ALL NATIVE AMERICAN PEOPLES ON BEHALF OF THE UNITED STATES OF AMERICA; AND BE IT FURTHER

RESOLVED, THAT A COPY OF THESE RESOLUTIONS BE FORWARDED BY THE CLERK OF THE SENATE TO THE CLERKS OF THE SENATE AND HOUSE OF REPRESENTATIVES OF THE UNITED STATES.

SENATE, ADOPTED, JUNE 22, 2006..

PRESIDENT OF THE SENATE

CLERK OF THE SENATE

OFFERED BY:

SENATOR STEVEN C. PANAGIOTAKOS

SENATOR EDWARD M. AUGUSTUS, JR.

SENATOR STEVEN A. BADDOUR

SENATOR HARRIETTE L. CHANDLER

SENATOR SUSAN FARGO

SENATOR THERESE MURRAY

SENATOR ROBERT O'LEARY

SENATOR STANLEY C. ROSENBERG

SENATOR DIANNE WILKERSON

Resolution of Apologies to Native American Peoples on Behalf of the United States

(Left to right) Apostle Najem, Chief Slyfox, Dr. Bigpond, Senator Panagiotakas

Dr Bigpond giving Apostle Najem the name Strong Wings

Apostle Najem with mother Em Raffoul

Dr. Elias Malki

Raymond Abou Assaly and Apostle Najem (2016)

Raffoul Najem (far right) during High School years

Bible School students (Raffoul Najem furthest left)

Arabic Christian men's conference (Raffoul Najem center)

CHAPTER

2

THE WAR IN LEBANON

One day, after a cease-fire had been negotiated, I was at home with my mother, relaxing with a book. Suddenly, I heard the sounds of loud knocks and screaming in the apartment hallways. As I went to the door, my heart sank. I knew something bad was about to happen. I opened the door to find six militiamen fully armed. "Are you Raffoul Najem?" they demanded. I could barely breathe. "Yes," I quivered. "Come with us now." They spit their words out at me impatiently. "You are wanted at the office of Fatah." We walked down the stairs and past my neighbors who were still screaming in fear. The blaring sun and the sound of growling engines met us as we stepped outside. I squinted to see three Jeeps full of angry militiamen. They forced me into the back of one of the Jeeps as Muslim Palestinians fired rapidly into the air in an attempt to drive away my neighbors who had followed us outside to beg for my life. However, my advocates would not be deterred, and hundreds of men and women forced their way to the jeep and surrounded it in a rescue attempt. An older gentleman, a friend of the family, tried to bargain with the men, offering what little he had for my life, but they would not entertain any bribes, and they slapped him hard across the face. I turned my head and looked to the back of Jeep and saw my mother with tears pouring down her face, clinging onto the gate with every ounce of strength she could muster. She desperately pleaded with them not to take me, and one of the gunmen struck her repeatedly with his rifle, but my mother was a strong woman and she would not be deterred. I wanted to fight, but I was powerless, but watching my mother's perseverance gave me enough strength to reach out and pull her into the truck with me. She climbed into the back of the Jeep and sat defiantly next to me, blood dripping down her face from the rifle's wound. Seeing her tenacity, the gunman spit in disgust but motioned for the jeeps to head out.

There was so much commotion when we arrived at the Captain's office. People were shuffling in and out of the door in what looked like an endless circle. As we walked through the halls, I could hear guards yelling as they interrogated their prisoners. Outside the window, machine guns shot into the air to threaten my friends and relatives who were trying to storm into the building and demand my release. I worried for my mother as she and I had been separated at the door of the building, and I knew that she would not relent easily. I was led to the end of a long, ominous hallway and was directed into the Captain's office. He was a young man, likely in his early thirties with dark, curly hair and rugged features. He was fervently cleaning his handgun, his brow furrowed in frustration, and as we walked in, he peered up at me, cursed, and spit on the floor. I knew I should have been overwhelmed with fear as I watched him, but instead, I felt the peace of God. In a surge of boldness, I looked straight in the Captain's eye and said confidently, "Do not touch me. It will not go well with you if you do. I am a man of God." He stared at me for a long minute and I watched his eyes as he battled between anger and fear. He stared at me in disdain for a long moment, but like a soldier focused on his task, I held his gaze. Finally, he broke the silence and snarled to the guard standing by, "Take him away! Let him go home. We have no need for him here." I heard familiar voices in the hallway and suddenly, my mother appeared with a charge of my angry relatives behind her. The Captain erupted in anger and screamed, "Momma, go home! There is no need for you to bring all these people. I released your son, he is free to go, and so are you!" He dismissed us with a flick of his wrist and turned his focus back to cleaning his gun.

We left the headquarters as quickly as possible. On our way, we met my uncle and two brothers who had heard the news of my capture and had been running in the streets crying. They thought I was gone forever as this had been the fate of so many others. They couldn't believe their eyes when they saw us come around the corner covered in dust and sweat, my mother dancing circles of joy around me. Our scary evening turned into one of dancing and rejoicing. When we arrived home, we found our house packed with concerned neighbors who welcomed me back with kisses and treats to enjoy. All evening, friends shook my hand, hugged me, and kissed my face. However, I could see the worry in their eyes. I knew what they were thinking, because I was thinking it too: "Who, or what, is next?"

July of 1976 marked three full years of civil war for the nation of Lebanon. Thousands of Christians and Muslims had been slaughtered. Beirut, a beautiful city once known as the "Paris of the Middle East," was now filled with crumbled buildings destroyed by fire from the missiles that flew overhead daily. The city was divided in half: East Beirut held the majority of the city's Christian population, and West Beirut where I lived was ruled by Muslims. Lebanon's deadly civil war was due to self-centered leaders who caused economic instability throughout the country, forcing many families to new lands in search of peace and employment. I was one among the many young men who decided to run away to save his life. I made that decision the day I was kidnapped and miraculously released. Almost without exception, Christians did not come back after being taken, and every other Christian I knew who was kidnapped was returned to their family in pieces. Sadly, it wasn't just the Muslim resistance who committed such atrocities. Christians responded in kind towards Muslims in their area of control.

The flow of trade was limited to the dividing line that separated the city. Due to this, some items became difficult to acquire. Some opportunists took advantage of the situation, and they made a living smuggling items back and forth between West and East Beirut. Unfortunately, many smugglers lost their lives while crossing the border, and my cousin was one of the casualties. He was smuggling propane tanks into our side of the city when a sniper struck him. That was how fleeting life was in those days— here one day and gone the next. Our local newspaper Al-Nahar reported a story of how one bullet killed an entire family. A young man went on a quest to get medicine for his baby brother who was ill, and while he was on his way, he was shot dead by a sniper. As it turned out, the sniper was the young man's other brother who had been hired to fight for the opposition, something that occasionally happened as desperation pushed people to accept any work they could find. Since the medicine was never obtained, the baby brother also died, and when the shooter realized the man he killed was his brother, he committed suicide. Their horrifying story was on the front page titled "One Bullet Kills Entire Family." Everyone we knew was affected by a heartbreaking story like this.

For six months, all the stores were closed, and we were left without running water or electricity. As the sole provider for my family, it was my responsibility to find water for our home. Transporting water for a large family was no easy task, so I built a wagon from neighborhood scraps and my mother cleaned out some empty gasoline jugs that I had gathered from around the city. I heard about a well that was working in West Beirut where we lived, so I headed off with my wagon in tow. When I arrived at the well, I found about twenty people already standing in line with their gasoline jugs and buckets. Initially, I thought they were waiting in line to fill their jugs, but I quickly realized the true cause of the delay. A sniper was positioned on the east side of the city within perfect shooting distance of our west side well. He let his rifle loose on the well in a consistent loop:

BANG! One, two, three, four, five- BANG! BANG! BANG!...

I got in line behind a middle-aged man with deep worry lines etched in his bronzed forehead. My heart sank when I realize that the group was counting the seconds between gunshots, memorizing the sequence so they could calculate the safest route to the well.

One, two, three- BANG! One, two, three, four, five- BANG! BANG! BANG! The gunfire flew like deadly, red laser beams across the open space. I kept my eyes on the old, rusty water pump in the far right side of the courtyard and calculated in my head how many steps it would take to get to the other side. The water pump gleamed in the distance like a diamond in the sun, promising life to all within its reach. My palms were sweating, making the stained, white plastic container slip in my hands.

We memorized the sniper's firing sequence: three seconds, one shot; five seconds, three shots; seven seconds, two shots. We calculated that our best chance would be to run after the three shots, giving us a full seven seconds to reach the other side. I watched as one person after another gathered their courage and ran as fast as they could to the well. The rest of us waited along the grey, crumbling wall lining the other side of the courtyard and counted the sequence out loud so the runner would know how much time was remaining.

When my turn came, I dug my toes into the gravel and took a few deep breaths. My heart beat so loudly in my head that I thought for sure the sniper would hear it echoing across the courtyard.

After the next sequence of three shots, I launched into a full speed sprint across the open courtyard. I could hear my partner counting out the sequence to me, his booming voice echoing back from the courtyard wall. The empty gasoline container slapped loudly against my thighs, and at seven seconds exactly, I slid into the dust alongside the water pump.

I filled the water container in record time, sealing off the liquid gold with a dirty black twist top. I knew the run back would be the hardest part as we had been standing in the hot, Beirut sun for hours, and I had used all of my remaining energy to get to the well. So, I closed my eyes and thought of my mother, as I often did in moments like this. I thought of her smile, her unruly brown hair, and her comforting smell of olive oil and lemon. I pictured her as she so often was, leaning over our old, tired, propane stove, nervously heating and reheating the mujaddara (a traditional Middle Eastern dish of cooked lentils and rice) stirring and singing gently under her breath. Thinking of her gave me the peace and strength that I needed to run back across the courtyard.

This remained our only way to get water for months. I went to that courtyard and waited in line once a week and it always took me half the day to get my jugs filled. The sniper was always there.

By 1975, the civil war had escalated to include foreign armies as well. The city was in total chaos. Thousands had died, thousands more had been displaced, and hundreds of buildings were completely destroyed. Beirut, once a beautiful jewel of the Middle East, had been turned it into an empty, smoldering city of grey concrete and ash, filled with bullet and bomb holes. From the outside, it appeared completely uninhabitable, but we were still there, surviving the best we could. The city was still divided in half, and international travel was only permitted from the east side of the city. By this point in the war, it was completely forbidden to cross the line that divided the city, called the green line. This new ordinance trapped those of us on the west side of the city. So I began to pray, asking God to help me develop a plan to escape the country.

By the time I was 22, I had lost all of my jobs, and there was no work available anywhere. One day, I was sitting on a balcony looking across the street at an empty piece of land. Since the war had put an end to the collection of garbage, people were beginning to leave their trash everywhere, and this particular lot was becoming the area dump. I hated to see my neighborhood overrun with the sights and smells of everyone's garbage, so I decided to clean it up. I gathered five young people from the neighborhood including my brothers Eli and George, and together, we dug a deep hole in the middle of the lot. With chemicals we obtained from the drug store, we burned the trash and purified the lot of any remaining bacteria.

After we finished cleaning the lot, I started to think about what we could do on that lot to make some money, and I had the idea to turn it into a falafel shack. Since all of the restaurants had been closed down due to the war, I knew that we could be successful if we could just find a way to get it started. There were some ceramic tiles left over at the church from previous renovations, so I brought them to the lot and laid them on the ground to make a floor. Next, my brother and I scavenged the neighborhood for some tin and a couple of two by fours, which we used to erect a small, makeshift shack. I was determined to have the best falafel in our neighborhood, so I took a chance and ventured to the home of the recently widowed, Assyrian wife of an old man who used to own a very popular falafel restaurant. She answered the door dressed completely in black, indicating that she was still in mourning. As I expected, she initially hesitated to give me the recipe, but after some negotiating she agreed when I promised to hire her nineteen-year-old son, Paul, to work with me. Across the city, good work was impossible to find, and people were willing to sacrifice anything for the possibility of earning a wage.

Initially, we traded things that we had to pay for our ingredients such as beans and oil, but finding produce was our biggest challenge. We didn't have a refrigerator, so we could only buy ingredients for one day at a time, and the only fresh produce available was sold from trucks that would come into the neighborhood at random times and locations. Every morning, we prayed for God to direct us as we walked around the neighborhood with our makeshift wagon in tow until we stumbled on a truck selling the produce we needed. We knew our venture was a gamble, yet I felt that God had led me to this decision, and I trusted that He would come through for me.

My mother knew how to make bread, so we built a little brick oven and gathered wood from the neighbors for fire. The bread she made is called markouk (a type of unleavened flat bread) and when it is done well, it is paper thin and extremely delicious.

It is normally made over a fire on a wok, but since we didn't have a wok, my mother bent a frying pan. Everyone loved her bread so much that years later, when she finally immigrated to the United States, she brought that wok with her.

The most difficult part of the process was grinding the beans and vegetables, as there was no electricity. So, we had to use a large hand crank grinder. Once our ingredients were prepared, my brother fried the falafel, and I made the sandwiches and collected the money. With all of us working together, our little operation ran very well, and soon the neighborhood was buzzing about our falafel. We charged one lira (Lebanese currency) a sandwich, which was considered expensive at the time. Before the war, restaurants sold them for only a quarter of a lira per sandwich, but because we made our own bread, people happily paid the extra charge. We opened the shack for only three hours a day, and we were so successful that we consistently sold out of sandwiches. I made more money in one week at our falafel stand than I was making in a whole month at my other two full time jobs combined.

Unfortunately, no matter how well we were doing, the threat of war was always on our minds. Our neighborhood had one building with an underground shelter in it that had been initially built to escape from earthquakes, and everyone in the neighborhood used that shelter. Whenever the bombs started falling, hundreds of us would come running from all directions to huddle tightly together in that dark shelter, so even the last person could squeeze in. Even though we were all afraid, we found ways to make it fun by telling stories and jokes, and in this way, we created strong relationships with the people in our community.

One evening, we were so busy at our falafel stand with a long line of people waiting for sandwiches that we failed to hear the familiar buzzing of impending disaster in the air. However, we couldn't ignore the blinding flashes of light and deafening explosions as bombs started falling from the sky, so we immediately left everything where it was and ran to the shelter to hide. After the threat was over, we went back to our stand and saw that we had lost everything. Determined to not be defeated, we cleaned up what we could and returned home resolved to start over again the next day.

CHAPTER

3

ESCAPE FROM LEBANON

Chapter 3: Escape From Lebanon

Three months after I started the falafel stand, God made a way for my brother and I to escape Lebanon. Prior to this, Dr. Malki had helped me try to obtain a visa to the United States several times, but up until this point, all of our efforts had failed. During this time, my youngest brother, George, worked as an accountant for a company that distributed newspapers from West to East Beirut. Since no one was allowed to cross from one side of the city to the other, they devised this strategy. Late at night, a Muslim driver named Ali in the West would take his Datsun pickup truck full of newspapers to the Lebanese National Museum, which was located on the Green Line (the line that separated East and West Beirut). A Christian driver would be waiting there with his empty truck. Then, the two men would simply swap trucks, sending the newspapers to be freely distributed throughout East Beirut. George made a deal with Ali that in exchange for two hundred dollars, Ali would smuggle my brother Eli and I across the Green Line in his truck bed along with the newspapers. We had no idea what we would do once we crossed the Green Line, or even where we would be going, but we knew that the only way to get a passport and leave Lebanon was through East Beirut. So we decided to take one step at a time and trust God to guide us along the way.

Eli and I lay down in the bed of his pickup truck and Ali covered us from head to toe with newspapers. I was terrified, but I couldn't help myself from peeking through a crack in the papers. The streets along the Green Line were almost completely destroyed. We passed building after building, once strong and productive, now windowless and burnt to an empty shell. Electrical wires hung over us as we swerved around enormous potholes and piles of burning rubber tires. The smell of trash, death, and smoke was so overwhelming that it made my eyes sting. The guards at the Green Line were fully armed, their machine guns gleaming in the sunlight. One of the guards must have seen me move under the papers, and my anxiety peaked as I heard him say to the driver, "Do you think we are stupid? We see the man in the back." Panic-stricken, Eli and I watched the guard and driver exchange some words and money. They let us go. To this day, I have no idea why.

My aunt lived in East Beirut, so thankfully, we had somewhere to stay once we crossed the line. While there, we also met up with a friend named Mary who told me that Dr. Malki was visiting Lebanon and he was in the area. I was thrilled, as I had not seen Dr. Malki in two years, so we quickly made plans to see him the next day. My heart jumped when I saw Dr. Malki again. Seeing him was further confirmation that God was truly with us and that He had ordained our escape. I had not heard from Dr. Malki in over a year, and I could barely contain my joy at seeing my spiritual father standing alive and healthy in front of me. Tears fell to my cheeks as I ran to embrace him, and I could feel hope renew in my heart once again. There was much to discuss, and we spoke about what had happened to West Beirut and how the civil war had destroyed all of our dreams for our future in Lebanon. We thanked God that we had survived up until that point and together, we dreamed up new ideas for a bright future for Lebanon and the Middle East once the war was over.

Dr. Malki introduced us to his friend Dr. Larry Ward who was the founder of the Food for the Hungry Organization. He was in Beirut organizing the arrival of ships carrying food and medicine for Lebanese Christians. Dr. Malki and Dr. Ward wanted me to stay in Lebanon to help with their distribution and represent the organization in the Middle East, but I knew I needed to leave the country. There was no hope or future for me there anymore. It was no longer the home that I knew and loved. So, with tears I pleaded to them, "I have to leave Lebanon and go to America! Please help me!" Dr. Ward was a very compassionate man and he convinced Dr. Malki that it was in our best interest to leave the country. He helped us leave the country, generously paying for all of our travel expenses.

The Cyprian Airport was the only way out for the Lebanese people as the war had forced our airports to close for international travel, so we had to first travel by boat from Beirut to Cyprus. Eli and I got our passports in East Beirut, and we left the country on a fishing boat headed for the island of Cyprus. There were about seventy-five people on the boat including Dr. Malki and Dr. Ward who were now on their way back to the United States. We were informed that the trip to Cyprus would take about eight hours, but it took our boat sixteen hours because the sea was raging with such intensity that our captain lost his way. I had such severe seasickness that I was vomiting constantly. I felt so horrible that I wished I had stayed in Beirut and died by a bullet instead. Dr. Ward had compassion for me, and he gave the captain four hundred dollars to let me stay down below the deck in the Captain's quarters. His quarters were so deep below the deck of the boat that the rocking calmed, and I was able to lay down on a bed and rest.

My brother and I did not have visas to leave Cyprus, so when we arrived in Cyprus, Dr. Ward made a phone call to a friend, a Greek Cyprian resident who quickly came to get us. He brought us to an American church building that had been abandoned due to the Cyprian Civil War going on at the time. I had not heard about this war, and it was very distressing to us to be in yet another city scarred with the evidence of vicious combat. There were bullet holes everywhere and buildings were abandoned and destroyed. I felt like a mouse running in an endless maze. No matter where I went, I could not escape war.

We stayed about fifteen days in the abandoned church building, and we were living on very little with only one mattress, a refrigerator, and a stove. Almost every penny that we had was spent on groceries, and we tried to make it stretch as long as we could because we did not know when or even if anyone would come back to help us. Our days were spent people-watching and listening as streams of people walked by the church speaking in a language we did not understand. The Cyprians watched us as well, and they stared at us constantly. We knew they were trying to figure out who we were and why we were there. We did not have a television or a telephone, and there were no visitors to the abandoned church, so the days dragged by as we waited for word from Dr. Ward or one of his American friends. Cooking became a joy to me during those days, and simply finding resourceful ways to create something delicious out of our meager ingredients felt empowering to me. Even so, we were tortured every night by our neighbor who regularly barbecued shish kebab just downwind of us. We salivated at the smell and dreamed of just one delicious bite, but we did not dare spend our money on meat, a costly luxury.

By the time we reached day fifteen, we lost all hope that we would hear from Dr. Ward again. We were stressed and worried as we were almost out of money and didn't have enough funds to afford a return trip to Lebanon. Just as we were contemplating our options, we heard a knock at the door! We ran to open it and found an American Marine standing there. With my limited English, I was able to understand that Dr. Ward had sent a telegraph to the American Embassy in Cyprus. He told them about our situation and requested their help.

At the American embassy, Eli and I stood before the Councilor apprehensive, knowing that his decision would determine the rest of our lives. Sitting behind the desk was a large, stone-faced, African American man. He was not happy that we were in his office and he grouchily asked us, "Why are you here?" I was concerned that my limited amount of English would not be sufficient to communicate clearly, but somehow he understood everything I said without a problem. "We would like visas to the United States," I told him. This was not my first time applying for a visa, a fact that the Councilor reminded me of vehemently. "You applied in Beirut two years ago and you were denied. Why should I grant you a visa now?" He stared at me with his hands folded on top of our shiny new passports. I was nervous, but I held my ground and responded firmly, "It was not God's timing before, but it is God's timing now. It is His will that you give me a visa today." The Councilor stared at us with confused eyes, and it was clear that he had no idea what to make of us. After an hour of interviewing, he sighed and said, "Look son, God has nothing to do with this." He paused and looked at our faces before shifting his gaze down to our passports, his fingers mindlessly thumbing the pages in contemplation. Finally he spoke. "Dr. Ward was a college colleague of mine, and I have a lot of respect for him. If he was not sponsoring you, you would never see a visa to the United States." I will never forget the sound of his stamp over our passports. It was the sweetest sound in the world, and Eli and I breathed a huge sigh of relief. I exclaimed, "Thank you, Sir! See? It is God's will!" The Councilor cracked a wide smile, and with a tilt of his head, he laughed and said,

"Get out of here." We left his office leaping and laughing! We looked at our visas over and over in complete shock, unable to believe what our eyes were seeing. God had made a way.

We headed straight to the post office to make a collect call to our older sister Amal, who was already living in the United States. Five years prior, Amal had married a Lebanese American man named Raymond, and the two moved to the United States and were living in Methuen, Massachusetts. Raymond worked very hard and had become a successful car dealer working for Subaru in Salem, New Hampshire. We had initially hoped they would be able to sponsor our visas to the United States. However, we quickly learned that this would be impossible as Amal had not yet obtained her American citizenship. We were truly counting on God to sponsor our travel to the United States every step of the way.

Amal answered our collect call and was relieved to know that we were safe and thrilled to hear that we would be meeting her soon. She immediately wired us airline tickets and we used our last five Cyprian pounds to pay for the taxi to the airport. We bounced up to the British Airways desk, unable to contain our excitement. Unfortunately, it did not last long because when we arrived, the ticket agent informed us that while we did have tickets, we did not have confirmed flight reservations. He explained that there was only one flight per week that left Cyprus for London, and it was that evening at eleven. Since we did not have reservations, we were not guaranteed a seat on that flight and may need to wait until the following week. I was so exhausted and emotionally drained that I screamed at the agent, "No one told us that we needed reservations, Sir!" We did not have a penny to our name, not even enough to get to get us back to the church building. The agent was patient with us and with an understanding sigh, he said, "OK, I'll tell you what. Go over there and have a seat in that corner and wait." He didn't tell us what to wait for, but we did as we were told. We sat despairingly on two old, weathered chairs in the corner, and I looked at Eli's face. He had tears in his eyes, so I told him, "Do not fear. Jesus will perform a miracle. He will take care of us." It felt good to speak out in faith, as I needed the encouragement as much as he did.

Eleven o'clock came and went and we watched heartbroken as the plane loaded with passengers. We almost gave up hope, but then, at 11:05, we heard our names paged through the loud speakers. We ran to the gate where the agent smiled and told us, "Well, this has never happened before, but two people did not show up for the flight, so you two can have their seats." We were like children on Christmas morning and we laughed and giggled all the way to our seats. Our fellow travelers must have thought that we were crazy, but we didn't care. At twenty-four and twenty-two years old, this was our first time on a plane!

Our flight itinerary had a twenty-four hour layover in London. Since we were unsure of what we should do, we asked a customs officer who told us we would need a visa to stay in London. I felt myself start to panic as I told the officer that we were not informed that we needed a visa. He looked me straight in the eyes and asked, "What do you do for a living?" I wasn't sure why he was asking, but I told him I was a preacher of the gospel. After a long pause he responded, "Okay, follow me," and he took us by the hand to the British Airways booth. The agent was not happy that the airline failed to inform us that we would need a visa, and he made a big, dramatic scene expressing his disdain to the agents at the booth. He insisted they make it right and demanded that they give us a voucher to stay the night in a hotel. They reluctantly agreed and gave us a voucher to stay the night at a gorgeous, local hotel for free. God had come through for us again, and we were so grateful. Our hotel room was beautiful, and it had a nice, clean bed and a shower with hot water. It had been weeks since we had a hot shower; it felt so amazing. I thought I had died and gone to heaven.

Raffoul (left) and brother Eli Najem

Young Pastor Raffoul Najem and Dr. Elias Malki

Sister Amal in the U.S.A

CHAPTER

4

LIFE IN UNITED STATES

Chapter 4: Life In United States

The next day, we boarded the flight to Boston without any delays. As we began our descent to Boston, I remember looking out of the plane window at the harbor below and feeling many mixed emotions. I was crying tears of joy at the opportunity we had been given and at the chance to live our lives safe from war. However, I also cried tears of sadness as I realized that life as we knew it in our home in Lebanon was over. Life flashed before my eyes as I looked out that window- my past, my present and my future, and I contemplated what this new world would have for me. Eli and I caught eyes and I could read the same excitement and fear on his face. We talked nervously about what we thought America would be like, but since the only reference that we had to life in America was from the television shows Bonanza and Peyton Place, those were the only scenarios we could imagine. We were told we would "find dollars on the streets," so for two young men coming from the brink of poverty, we literally felt as if we were moving to the proverbial "land of milk and honey."

It was August 15, 1976 at 3:00 p.m. when we arrived in the United States, and we walked out into the blazing sun and onto American soil for the first time with only fifteen cents and a small bag of clothes between us. It was all of our earthly possessions, but we didn't care. At that moment, we were the richest men in the whole world.

Amal and Raymond and a few of their friends were waiting for us in the terminal. Words cannot describe all the feelings we experienced that day: joy, sadness, curiosity, fear, and relief. We were overwhelmed by the simple things like driving down the highway, the width of which felt like the size of a city compared to the small narrow paths, which we were used to traveling on in Lebanon. We were determined to adjust to American life as quickly as possible, and within a few days, Eli and I taught ourselves how to drive and used our school IDs to obtain driver's licenses. Raymond helped us to secure jobs at his car dealership and I learned how to sell cars very quickly. I was a natural salesman, so after only three weeks, I was able to return the five hundred dollars that I had borrowed from Dr. Malki.

We loved our new lives, but as time passed, our honeymoon in America waned. Reality set in, and I realized that this new world was not at all what I thought it would be. It was a struggle to adjust to the differences between my simple life in Lebanon and the extravagance, that surrounded me in America. There were many days that I felt bored and I was surprised at how secular the American culture was. Hospitality plays a vital role in the Lebanese culture, so I was used to having close relationships with my neighbors and friends where there was no need to call before a visit to their home. It was daily custom to drop by each other's homes to fellowship, eat, play games, laugh, and pray together, and I couldn't understand why it seemed that the people in my new world rarely visited each other. I missed the warm greetings of strangers while walking the streets and the beautiful way my people respected and honored the elderly generation. We may have been poor, but we had laughter, stories and genuine fellowship among us all the time. Even in the midst of war, people selflessly helped and served each other joyfully without the anxiety of insurance payments or the fear of being sued. At twenty-four years of age, I was shocked to see how males and females interacted in public. I would never have dared to even touch a female, never mind kiss her! It seemed so disrespectful. I struggled to reconcile the culture that I saw around me with the way that I had been raised. Everything was different in America, and I often found myself so homesick, I would cry. I wanted to run home, but I knew there was no way for me to return. I still needed to gather enough money to save my family from living in the constant danger of war. Besides, I knew that the Lebanon I knew and loved would never be the same. To this day, I can still be moved to tears when I consider the heartbreak of all that has been lost in my beloved country.

Desperate to fill my aching void of companionship, I visited a few churches searching for like-minded people, but I never felt welcome. No one cared to say hello to a foreigner like me. I felt utterly alone. One day, as I was sitting alone in the show room of the dealership crying to the Lord about my desperate need for fellowship, a customer came into the store. I noticed immediately that he had a bumper sticker on his car about Jesus, so I asked him where he went to church. He was very friendly and happy to chat about his small, home fellowship church in Salem, New Hampshire. I didn't know it then, but the moment he gave me his church's address would prove to be an important turning point in my life.

I visited the church the first chance that I had and immediately loved it. The people were kind, and they loved and embraced me as their own. I became a very close friend to the leader of the group, a very genuine man of God named Ron Rosi, and in less than five months, I became the leader of the singles group. Every week, about thirty of us would come together to learn and study God's Word. We were fellowshipping daily, and every Friday night, we would go to the beach, build a bonfire, and stay until midnight worshiping God with a guitar.

Three years later, I went to Egypt and married Soheir, whom

I had met six years prior in one of our church conferences in Lebanon. After our first child Jennifer was born, my friend Ron introduced me to a man named John Purpura who was holding another small fellowship in his home in Westford, Massachusetts. It was there that I met Vi Whitcomb who would later play a very important role in my life. My wife and I visited this small congregation in early 1982, and we knew from our first visit that God had directed us there. We decided to shut down our fellowship in Salem and combine our groups into one church. I started preaching immediately, and even though our group was small, the relationships we built together were strong and genuine. Even early on, we recognized that relationship was the key to growing a powerful, charismatic church family. I finally found my home in the United States and started to forget my old life in Lebanon.

At last, I felt like an American, but it wasn't until I visited Lebanon for the first time after three years of living in the United States that I officially decided to start the paperwork to become an American citizen. That trip really opened my eyes to the extreme cultural decline the war had caused in my country. Human life in Lebanon was no longer valued, and people killed each other over small, foolish arguments. Only the rich and famous had the ability to pay for justice, and corruption was rampant. Poverty was everywhere, but the middle class was the most miserable of all. Families constantly fought for a better life and valuable education for their children without any way to make this possible. It was like being stranded on a desert island with a perfect view of the mainland in the distance, but no possible way to cross the stormy seas that separate you. Every little thing presented obstacles, so that even the smallest tasks could overwhelm your entire day.

For example, one day during my visit, I offered to help pay an outstanding electric bill for my parents. In Lebanon, there was no way to pay your bill online or give a credit card number over the phone, so we had to go to the post office, stand in line, and pay it in person. I left early in the morning, hopeful that I would be able to secure a spot toward the beginning of the line. Unfortunately, by the time I arrived, it was already fifty people deep, starting in the lobby and snaking its way outside and around the corner of the building. I sighed and took my place at the back of the line. I could almost hear the concrete walls sizzling in the blazing Middle East sun. Men mumbled in warm conversation and women in dark "abayas" fanned their sweaty faces with stacks of damp paper bills.

We waited all day in that steamy line, holding places for each other when we needed to run to the bathroom or grab a bag of chips from the vendor across the street. I breathed a sigh of relief when I reached the door to the post office and saw that there were only five people left ahead of me. Glancing at my watch, I thanked God that there was still plenty of time to pay my parents' bill before the post office closed. The line moved forward one space and I stepped across the building's threshold. Three years in the United States had made me accustomed to the comfort of air conditioning, and I half expected to feel its icy blast when I entered the room. Instead, I was met with only more stifling heat. I tapped my foot and wiped a bead of sweat from my upper lip as two people ahead of me left at the same time, allowing me to take three giant steps forward. I reached into my pocket for my wallet and my mother's crumpled electric bill. One more customer squeezed past the line and out the door as I counted my money and arranged it in my hand with the bill. I wanted to be ready to pay and end the nightmare of an errand as quickly as possible. The lone customer ahead of me walked forward and slid his bill across the counter, but the attendant ignored him and instead grabbed some paperwork and a pack of cigarettes that were piled on the counter next to him, and walked away. We looked at each other, a sinking feeling in our gut. We knew what was coming. One minute later, a young teenager came over and informed us that the attendant was closing early to go on a coffee break and that we would need to come back tomorrow. No apologies and no warning. We grumbled to each other as we left, but each of us knew it was no use to complain. It was just the way life was in Lebanon. I walked home with my head in my hands and contemplated all the frustrations and struggles that I had just experienced on my brief visit back to Lebanon. All at once, my eyes were opened to the beauty and ease of raising a family in the United States, and I decided right then and there that the United States would be my new home forever. I couldn't wait to proudly call myself an American.

God was with me in America just like He was with Joseph in Egypt. With His help, in only ten years' time, I went from being a poor man with only fifteen cents in my pocket, hardly speaking English, to a very successful co-owner of a multi-million-dollar Subaru dealership. I worked my way up from salesman, to sales manager, to general manager, to the president of the corporation, and finally, to a proud co-owner along with my brother Eli. For the first few years, we worked as much as we could, averaging about eighty hours a week so we could save enough to bring our whole family to the United States. It didn't take long for us to reach our goal and soon we and our Mom, Dad, younger brother, and two sisters were all living together again under one roof. We were safe, clean, and respected, and we felt enormous pride that we were able to provide this for our family.

Soon after, I was married, and as the years passed, my wife Soheir and I grew our family by three wonderful children. I had a steady income and was running a home fellowship at my house. Life was good, but deep inside, I still felt an empty, nagging void. Something was missing. I knew that this was not God's best for me, and I couldn't ignore the voice of the Holy Spirit calling me to something else. The inner turmoil was too much to bear and one day while I was crying to God, I felt him say to me, "Raffoul, be quiet. Why do you keep crying to me? If you don't like what you are doing, quit!"

At that point, the economy shifted and our business started to suffer. We needed to come up with an average of $25,000 by eleven o'clock every morning just to cover overdrafts. For two years every morning, Eli and I would pray, and every day God would provide. However, it didn't take long for me to realize that God's miraculous provision didn't necessarily mean that it was His will for me to stay.

I remembered my promise to God that I would preach His gospel to the nations, and deep in my heart, I knew that it was time for me to do what God was calling me to do. I spoke with my wife about my desire to go into full time ministry, and at first, she wasn't willing to let me make such a huge career change. But at midnight on New Year's Eve in 1989, God spoke to her and said "Let him go." I came home from church at about 1:00 am that morning, and I found her in our bed crying. She told me what God had said to her, and I instantly made the final decision to give up my career in the business world and go into full time ministry. The next day, I shared my heart and my wife's story with the elders of the church, and together, we rejoiced and thanked God for what He was doing and all the wonderful things to come. I officially became the Senior Pastor of Community Christian Fellowship later that month, and I have joyfully served the congregation from that moment on.

CHAPTER

5

BECOMING STRONG WINGS

In January of 1990, CCF was at its best, growing quickly from two hundred to five hundred people in just three years. During that time, a church of this size was considered a mega church by New England standards. As we were praying about what our next step would be as a church, my wife came to me with the idea of starting our own Christian school. She had met an Assemblies of God pastor and his wife who were working to pioneer Christian schools in inner cities, so she introduced them, and we met together a few times to glean insight from their years of experience. I knew that starting a school would be a massive undertaking and I wasn't convinced we could handle all that it would require. However, at Soheir's encouragement, the elders and I prayed together, and God confirmed that this was indeed the next step for our growing church. We established our school in September of 1991 and named it Community Christian Academy (CCA). We started CCA with about thirty-five students and because we only had five classrooms, we had to put three to four grades together in a room. We were determined to grow and knew God would honor our efforts. That first year, we only had one graduate, and the second year there were only two. Even though our growth was slow, it was steady, and year after year, God faithfully brought staff and students to our doors. Today, we have 185 students, and the school is still growing every year with some classes filling to capacity. All three of my children graduated from our academy, and now my oldest daughter Jennifer is the school's principal. She is an amazing leader and minister of Christian education. We are proud to offer quality, Christian education to both our church body and to the community in which God has placed us.

The year 1992 ushered in dark days as the church suffered a difficult and painful split. The man who was serving as our school principal caused dissension among our church family. When he eventually left to start his own church literally down the road from us, he took half of our members with him, even splitting some families and households.

It was a horrible time, and it brought us to our knees. For months, we did nothing but seek the face of God, praying that He would turn this heartbreaking situation into something beautiful. True to His character, God came through for us. We started to receive spiritual revelation after revelation, and it became the greatest time of growth for not only the church, but in my personal walk as well. One of the greatest things that happened during this time is that one of our school parents reached out to her pastor, Bishop Stanley Choate of NEP Ministries in Pelham, NH. Bishop Choate came to meet with me and offered great words of consolation and advice. A great friendship began that helped carry us through this storm. A series of powerful teachings on relationship and unity was born in these difficult days, and together, the leadership and church body made a commitment that a split would never take place again.

The time came for us to start the process of rebuilding our church, but we made a decision to approach it a different way this time. During this time, I attended a Promise Keepers pastor's conference in Philadelphia where about forty thousand pastors were gathered in unity for worship, intercession, and teaching. While I was there, I met an artist who was painting a picture he had titled "Keeper of the Flame." Centered in the painting was Christ with His arms outstretched toward a multi-ethnic group of people below him. They stood with heads lifted to heaven and eyes closed in reverent worship, and a single flame hovered over each of them, representing the fire of the Holy Spirit. The painting stirred something in my heart, so I bought it and hung it in my office as a daily reminder of God's vision for our church. God had given us a new direction, and we prayed that our church would become a multi-ethnic, multi-generational melting pot. At the time, we were almost an entirely white Caucasian congregation, but I wanted nothing more than to look out over our church and see a sea of different generations and nationalities looking back at me. It felt like an impossible task, but I knew it was God's vision for us, and He would be the one to bring the dream to reality. It only took us two years to rebuild our church, and I am proud to say that today, we truly are a multi-generational church family with over thirty-two nationalities represented.

As our church family increased in size, so did our need for space, forcing us to regularly move our congregation from location to location. Because of this, we were given the nickname "The Church on the Move." We finally settled in a large, 15,000 square foot industrial building that we leased for ten years. Slowly, the size of our church and demands of the ministry outgrew our location once again, and we started to pray that God would give us our own building, one that was at least double the size.

Senator Panagiotakos invited us to look into renting space in a beautiful fifty-year-old Jewish synagogue in the heart of our city called Temple Bethel. We went to view the building and saw that it was 45,000 square feet and had a full gymnasium and spacious kitchen. It was everything we were looking for and more, so we approached the leaders of the Hebrew congregation. From that point on, we met once a month for hours at a time to discuss how we could make this work for both parties.

It was just me—a Christian Arab—and their board of trustees, which was comprised of seven Jewish men. It took many hours of tense negotiations to sign a deal which allowed us to share the building with the Hebrew congregation of Temple Bethel. After a whole year of discussions, we finally came to a comfortable compromise, and I joked that we could have solved the Middle East crisis in the time we spent negotiating together. We decided to divide the building into three sections. We called the first section the Outer Court where we had the freedom to do whatever we needed, wherever we needed to do it, and the second was called the Holy Place where we shared space and followed an agreed upon combined calendar. The third was a small section of the building where we were not allowed to go called the Holy of Holies. Over the years, those Jewish men became good friends and to this day, I still receive invitations from them to celebrate the Passover meal at their homes. When we finally closed the deal, our congregation marched the three miles from our existing church building all the way to our new home at Temple Bethel. We shared the building for two years until the Hebrew congregation was ready to move on, and we purchased the building from them. We gave them a prominent location on the property to erect a large stone memorial in remembrance of the years they spent in the building, and members of the synagogue occasionally visit and leave flowers at the memorial.

Finally, after more than sixteen years of wandering from one building to another, we found a permanent home at Temple Bethel, right in the heart of our home city of Lowell, Massachusetts. We were thrilled because it was our dream to be able to serve the inner city. During this time, I was also in the midst of a sermon series entitled Bethel, which was about the story of Jacob's dream of a ladder that stood between heaven and earth. I shared how God had brought us to Bethel spiritually, not knowing that He had planned for us to occupy Temple Bethel physically. I put a ladder in the sanctuary and had people climb up and down on it while I was preaching to symbolize the connection between what God was doing both spiritually and physically. It was an exciting time in our church's history.

Years passed and both CCF and CCA continued to grow steadily until another dark time arrived. My marriage had been under tremendous turmoil and eventually, we decided to separate, with the hope and prayer that with much hard work, we would be able to find a way to restore our relationship. I wish I could say that we found success, but sadly, we divorced in 2013. My divorce shook the foundation of the church, and a number of people chose to leave the church, some in very painful ways. I made the difficult decision to step down from my position, and I came very close to leaving the ministry altogether. However, I returned after one year due to the encouragement I received from my spiritual father Dr. Elias Malki, Faith Christian Fellowship International (our church's spiritual covering), and the elders of our church body. Their consistent support, prayers, and words of encouragement had a huge impact on restoring me to my role as pastor and ultimately, apostle.

Despite the horrible consequences of divorce and the ugliness that it so often brings, I can honestly say that I learned a big lesson from that difficult time. Divorce is not the end of life because we serve a God who is bigger than divorce. We serve a God who makes all things beautiful, one who can "restore the years that the locusts have eaten" (Joel 2:25). Our God loves second chances and has a never ending well of forgiveness.

My God is a God of new beginnings for all of His children. It amazes me to look back at what could have completely destroyed our church and my ministry and see that instead, God has used me to accomplish great and mighty things for His Kingdom. Today, Community Christian Fellowship is one large, extended church family spread over eight locations, and due to this multi-location expansion, we have recently changed our name to CCF Ministries. God has also used me with Dr. Cecilio Hernandez to co-found the Citywide Church of Greater Lowell, which consists of over a dozen churches of different denominations and ethnic groups working together to bless the City of Lowell. In May of 2016, I was led by the Holy Spirit to host the first "family reunion" of all of my spiritual sons and daughters currently serving in full time ministry all over the world. Over sixty people attended the event, and we had a wonderful time worshiping and celebrating the Lord together.

In October of 2016, Bishop Geoffrey Matoga, the father of one of my spiritual sons, Pastor Zenzo Matoga, came to preach at our Sunday morning service. His word was powerful and timely, and during his sermon, he prophesied over me, calling me an apostle of unity. I had been called an apostle prior to this, but it wasn't until Bishop Matoga prophesied over me and preached about the tremendous theological manifestations of apostolic ministry that my eyes were truly opened. One of our elders—Bishop David Karaya—a Kenyan and powerful man of God, stood up, took the microphone, and profoundly declared, "It is time to appoint our senior pastor Raffoul Najem as an apostle." He called Elder Vi to join him in praying over me and the whole church joined them. I understood in that moment the fullness of the principle of being appointed by the right spiritual authority—my elders and my covering. As they prayed, something profound took place in my heart, and it was equivalent to the feeling that I had when I accepted Christ and became born again. Their declaration resonated in me deeply, and for the first time, I was able to fully understand and gladly receive the appointment and anointing as apostle.

I give God all the glory for every good thing in my life. I am indescribably grateful to Him for His endless mercy and grace, for my loving children who are serving the Lord wholeheartedly, for my fellow church elders and friends who never gave up on me, and for CCF, a remnant of wonderful God-chasers and lovers of the kingdom of God.

I am Strong Wings. Not because of anything that I have done in and of myself. I am strong because the trials in my life have taught me to trust in the steadfast faithfulness of Christ. He is strong when I am weak, and it is His gentle wind that has raised me to places I never dreamed that I could reach. I was a teenager in a war torn city, a young man in a foreign land, a grown man facing life's daily challenges, and a pastor desperately seeking God's best for His people. Through it all, He was shaping me, molding me, and strengthening my wings so I could trust Him to carry me through the toughest storms and take me to the highest heights. Now, His wind is calling me again, beckoning me to new places and new challenges. In the distance, I can see a spiritual revolution arising, which will mark the last reformation of the Church before the second coming of the Lord. It is an exciting time, a time to come together and soar like eagles despite our differences and personal challenges. The wind of God is blowing again, the likes of which has never been seen before. It is a "Gentle Wind," (the Holy Spirit) and now I can confidently say, "I'm ready to soar this wind. I finally know who I am. I am Strong Wings, trusting Gentle Wind."

KEEPER OF THE FLAME painting

Laura and Joshua Najem, some of the first students to attend Community Christian Academy

Apostle Najem with daughters Laura (left) and Jennifer at the Fatherhood Reunion

The Apostolic anointing on Apostle Najem. (From left to right) Pastor Elvira "Vi" Whitcomb, Pastor Barbara Matoga, Bishop David Karaya and Bishop Geoffrey Matoga

Recipe for Najems' Lebanese Falafel

Najem's Lebanese Falafel Recipe

Ingredients:
2lbs – Dried chickpeas
2 – Onions
6 – Garlic cloves
1 Tbsp – Salt (or to taste)
1-2 Tbsp – Falafel spice (can be found at international markets)
1 tsp – Baking soda
Vegetable oil for frying

Equipment needed:
A deep pot
A slotting spoon for removing falafel from oil
A mortar and pestle (optional)
Cutting board
Chef knife
Grater
Food processor
Cheesecloth or fine mesh strainer
Falafel press (optional. Can be purchased online or at international markets.)

Directions:
1) Cover dried chickpeas two thirds of the way with water, and soak at least 8 hours or overnight. Drain chickpeas, rinse with hot water and place on a towel lined sheet tray to dry off as much as possible.

2) Put 2-3 inches of oil into deep pot on stove and begin heating to approximately 325 degrees Fahrenheit. While oil is heating, put chickpeas in a food processor and pulse to a medium coarse texture.

3) Using a mortar and pestle, grind up garlic cloves with ½ tsp of salt into a fine paste. (Alternately, you can do this by smashing the garlic on a cutting board with the flat part of your knife and, using the same flat side, scrape and mash the garlic and salt mixture back and forth until a fine paste forms.)

4) Using a fine grater, grate the onion and place onion pulp into a cheese cloth or fine mesh strainer. Squeeze out as much moisture as possible.

5) Combine all ingredients except the baking soda together and mix well until all are combined. Lastly, add the baking soda and mix again.

6) Test oil with a pinch of falafel mixture. If oil is bubbly, it is ready. Begin shaping falafel using a falafel press and release it into the oil. Do not fry more than 5-6 at a time to ensure that the oil doesn't cool. (Alternately, you can press the falafel by hand. Press 1.5 tbsp of mixture into slightly round disks measuring approximately 3/4 thick x 1 ¼ wide.) Fry falafel for 2-3 minutes or until a medium to dark color forms. Set on paper towel and sprinkle with a pinch of kosher salt. Let rest for a couple minutes as it will finish cooking through while it cools.

7) Serve immediately with fresh pita, shredded lettuce, diced tomatoes, radishes, and parsley. Top with a drizzle of taratour (a garlic tahini sauce which can be purchased online or at international markets).

Made in the USA
Columbia, SC
29 May 2018